The Exxon Valdez Oil Spill

PETER BENOIT

Children's Press®
An Imprint of Scholastic Inc.
New York   Toronto   London   Auckland   Sydney
Mexico City   New Delhi   Hong Kong
Danbury, Connecticut

Content Consultant
W. Scott Pegau, PhD
Research Program Director
Oil Spill Recovery Institute
Cordova, Alaska

Library of Congress Cataloging-in-Publication Data

Benoit, Peter, 1955–
   The Exxon Valdez oil spill/Peter Benoit.
      p. cm.—(A true book)
   Includes bibliographical references and index.
      ISBN-13: 978-0-531-20629-4 (lib. bdg.)   ISBN-13: 978-0-531-28998-3 (pbk.)
      ISBN-10: 0-531-20629-7 (lib. bdg.)   ISBN-10: 0-531-28998-2 (pbk.)
   1. Exxon Valdez Oil Spill, Alaska, 1989—Juvenile literature. 2. Oil spills—Alaska—Prince William
Sound Region—History—20th century—Juvenile literature. 3. Oil spills—Environmental
aspects—Alaska—Prince William Sound Region—History—20th century—Juvenile literature.
4. Tankers—Accidents—Alaska—Prince William Sound Region—History—20th century—Juvenile
literature. 5. Exxon Valdez (Ship)—Juvenile literature. I. Title. II. Series.

   TD427.P4B454 2011
   363.738'2097983—dc22   2010045929

All rights reserved. Published in 2011 by Children's Press, an imprint of Scholastic Inc.
Printed in China. 62
SCHOLASTIC, CHILDREN'S PRESS, A TRUE BOOK and associated logos are trademarks and/or
registered trademarks of Scholastic Inc.

1 2 3 4 5 6 7 8 9 10 R 18 17 16 15 14 13 12 11

Find the Truth!

Everything you are about to read is true *except* for one of the sentences on this page.

Which one is **TRUE**?

T or F The *Exxon Valdez* never sailed again after the 1989 spill.

T or F Oil companies made a deal with the Chugach to use their land.

Find the answers in this book.

EXXON VALDEZ
WILMINGTON DEL

Contents

1 Disaster on the Reef

What happened in Prince William Sound? 7

2 The Aftermath

Can spills ever be cleaned up? 17

THE **BIG** TRUTH!

Leaving It All Behind

Whatever happened to the *Exxon Valdez*? 26

3 Human Error

Was the spill the result of one
mistake, or many? 29

Sea animals, such
as seals, are at risk
in oil spills.

4

A worker checks the depth of the oil in the ground along the shore.

4 Responsibility

Was the *Exxon Valdez*
oil spill unavoidable? **37**

True Statistics **43**

Resources **44**

Important Words **46**

Index **47**

About the Author **48**

The *Exxon Valdez* disaster led Congress to pass new laws about transporting oil.

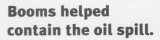

Booms helped contain the oil spill.

Oil from the *Exxon Valdez* quickly spread through the surrounding waters.

CHAPTER 1

Disaster on the Reef

On the evening of March 23, 1989, the *Exxon Valdez* left Valdez, Alaska. The ship was carrying 53.1 million gallons (201 million liters) of oil and was headed for Long Beach, California. Just after midnight on March 24, the *Exxon Valdez* **grounded** on a reef. The ship was damaged. Oil spilled from the ship, entering the cold Alaskan waters.

The *Exxon Valdez* oil spill is the second-largest marine oil spill in U.S. history.

The ship had grounded on Bligh Reef, not far from Bligh Island in Alaska's Prince William **Sound**. The damage to the ship was serious. Huge amounts of oil flowed into the waters of Prince William Sound. The *Exxon Valdez* lost almost 11 million gallons (41.6 million L) of oil. Most of the oil that the ship lost was spilled within six hours of hitting the reef.

This map shows where the *Exxon Valdez* ran aground and the extent of the oil spill.

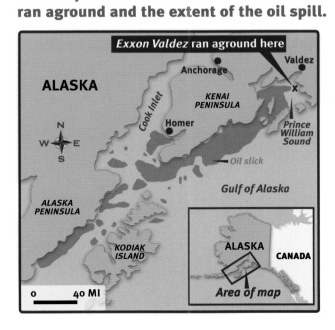

The amount of oil spilled could fill 17 Olympic-size swimming pools.

Oil spread farther and farther from the damaged ship.

The Oil Spreads

The *Exxon Valdez*'s captain, Joseph Hazelwood, sent word that the ship was in trouble. In the meantime, the oil continued to leak from the ship. At first, the oil mostly stayed around Bligh Reef. The oil floated in a large patch on the water's surface. Then, over the next several days, the oil began to drift south and west.

Pools of oil caused the waters around Prince William Sound to change color.

Three days after the accident, a storm blew into the area. It brought powerful winds. These winds quickly spread the oil over a much larger area. By March 30, the spill had spread 90 miles (145 kilometers) from the site of the accident. Eventually, it stretched all the way to Chignik, Alaska, 470 miles (750 km) away. About 1,300 miles (2,100 km) of shoreline were coated in oil.

Spring tides made the disaster even worse. Spring tides are much higher than normal tides. The higher water covers more of the coastline. After the *Exxon Valdez* had grounded, the oil was carried by the spring tides high onto the beach. The coast became covered in oil.

Thick, black oil quickly covered the Prince William Sound coastline.

Many believe that winter storms cleaned the coastline more effectively than workers did.

The effect of the spring tides was far reaching. Waves splashed oil onto rock faces that rose almost straight up. Oil sank into the sand along the coast. The oil that mixed into the sand was almost impossible to clean. Oil would be washed from one section of the shoreline, only to be carried elsewhere by the waves. All of these factors further complicated recovery efforts.

Workers dug holes to find out how deep the oil had soaked into the ground.

Some cleanup workers developed lung diseases from breathing oil fumes.

Rocks along the coastline were completely coated in oil.

Delayed Rescue

Officials on the shore learned of the accident almost immediately. For many reasons, however, response was delayed. Alyeska Pipeline Service Company, whose pipeline provided the *Exxon Valdez* with its oil, had a response **barge** for emergencies. This was out of service and could not be used.

The grounded ship's position was difficult to reach. Only helicopters or boats could reach it. Those in charge of rescue efforts had never planned for a disaster of this size. Not enough people or equipment were ready to act quickly and effectively. Response teams had to use what was available.

A helicopter flies above the *Exxon Valdez* to survey the oil spill.

Another Spill

On December 23, 2009, Bligh Reef was in the news again. The tugboat *Pathfinder* had struck a reef. This was the same reef that had grounded the *Exxon Valdez* 20 years before. Two damaged tanks of the *Pathfinder* contained 33,500 gallons (126,800 L) of diesel fuel. At the time, the tugboat was being used to check for ice to make sure ships could travel safely in the area.

Even a smaller oil spill, like the one from *Pathfinder*, can do great harm to the environment.

Cleanup workers used high-pressure water sprayers to blast oil from rocks.

CHAPTER 2

The Aftermath

Exxon Corporation, the oil company that owned the *Exxon Valdez*, took responsibility for much of the cleanup. Cleaning up the oil was somewhat trial and error. The size and location of the spill made recovery difficult. To make matters worse, the oil caused serious damage to the area's ecosystem. The oil killed many plants and animals immediately. Thousands more died during the weeks and months following the spill.

 Less than 10 percent of the spilled oil was ever recovered.

Cleanup Challenges

Crews tried to clean up the oil in different ways. Special chemicals were added to the water. They cause oil to break up into drops that sink or scatter in the water. But the waves were not very active, so the chemicals did not mix with the oil very well. This method was soon stopped. Controlled burning of the oil was also tried. The storm on March 27 mixed too much water into the oil for it to catch fire, though.

Airplanes spread chemicals to break up the oil.

18

Booms help to keep the spilled oil in one place.

Today, more than 50 miles (80 km) of boom is kept on hand in case of an oil spill.

Days after the accident, equipment for mechanical cleanup was finally available. **Booms** are floating structures that keep spilled oil from spreading farther. They were placed around the ship and near areas where fish eggs are hatched. Skimmers were then used to scoop up the oil floating on the water's surface. This method, however, had its own problems. Thick oil and **kelp**, a water plant, clogged the equipment.

About 10,000 workers and volunteers helped with the cleanup.

Lift machinery helped workers aim huge hoses high above the shore to spray water onto the oil-covered rocks.

Hot Water

Cleaning oil in the water is challenging. Removing oil from beaches isn't any easier. Officials decided to use pressure washing along the shores. One process involved spraying the rocky areas along the shoreline with hot water. This was meant to clean the rocks where oil had collected. Unfortunately, the process also killed many plants and animals that serve as food for other coastal sea life.

The hot water also killed important bacteria and fungi. Scientists later found that these tiny life-forms actually help break down and remove the oil. After learning of this, workers tried to use it to their advantage. On some beaches, the bacteria were encouraged to grow. This method was most effective where the oil cover was not too thick.

Oil-eating bacteria such as these can help break down oil.

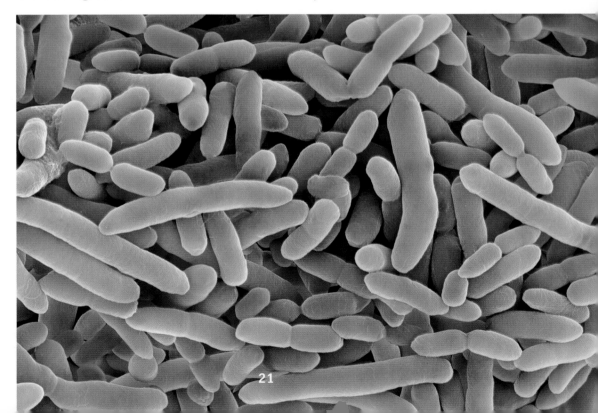

Even with the help of rescue workers, animals often died because of the oil spill.

Damaged Ecosystem

Loss of plant and animal life from pressure washing with hot water meant many creatures lost a food source. The oil also killed thousands of animals directly. Sometimes the oil coated fur or feathers. The animals became less able to keep warm in the cold Arctic weather. Animals were also poisoned by eating the oil. Some were trying to clean their fur. Other creatures ate animals coated in oil.

The oil had long-term effects as well. Animals sometimes went blind. They then had a harder time finding food and defending themselves. The oil also made it harder for many animals to reproduce. With fewer babies, populations decreased significantly.

Many workers helped clean the animals. Some animals were saved this way, but many could no longer survive in the wild.

Capturing, cleaning, and helping birds back into the wild cost an estimated $30,000 per bird.

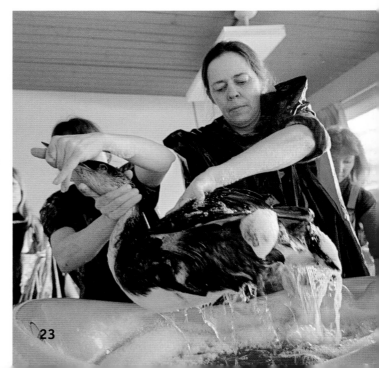

Oil-covered animals were cleaned with household dish soap.

The Cost

Hundreds of thousands of seabirds died immediately after the spill. Thousands of sea otters also died after trying to clean the oil from their fur. Harbor seals died by the hundreds. The pink salmon population decreased dramatically. Billions of salmon eggs were destroyed by the oil. Most animal populations are considered recovered, although the otters and some kinds of birds are not.

Some seals tried to escape the oily water by resting on nearby buoys.

24

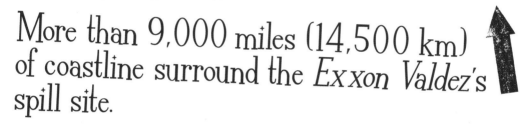

Before the oil spill, people traveled to Prince William Sound to fish and enjoy nature.

More than 9,000 miles (14,500 km) of coastline surround the *Exxon Valdez's* spill site.

The oil spill also damaged the area's economy, which is largely based on **commercial** fishing. Fish populations dropped. Fishers lost millions of dollars in the years right after the spill. With so few fish now living in the region's waters, sport fishers no longer visited. Tourists stopped coming, too. Businesses that depended on tourism lost money. Many had to close.

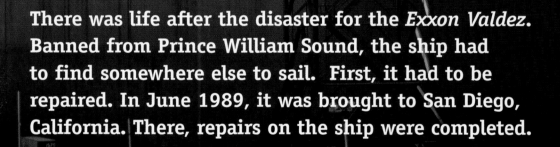

Leaving It All Behind

There was life after the disaster for the *Exxon Valdez*.
Banned from Prince William Sound, the ship had
to find somewhere else to sail. First, it had to be
repaired. In June 1989, it was brought to San Diego,
California. There, repairs on the ship were completed.

VALDEZ

In San Diego, more than 3 million pounds (1.4 million kilograms) of damaged steel was removed and replaced.

The repaired ship then sailed for SeaRiver Maritime, a company owned by Exxon. The ship carried oil across the Atlantic and Mediterranean for several years.

In 2008, the ship was sold to a Hong Kong company. The renamed ship, *Dong Fang Ocean*, is now used to carry metal ore from mines.

Workers used special oil-absorbing rags to wipe off rocks.

CHAPTER 3

Human Error

The *Exxon Valdez* oil spill did not have one cause. Many factors combined to create the disaster. Decisions and actions that took place months before helped lead up to it. Mistakes were made by the crew the night of the spill. They were also made by people who had never even seen the ship.

Exxon spent $2.1 billion on cleanup after the 1989 oil spill.

A working radar system is necessary to pilot large ships.

 Radar was first used on ships in the 1930s.

Sailing Blind

The Coast Guard was in charge of monitoring ships in Prince William Sound using **radar**. Radar is the use of radio waves to track the distance or location of objects. The waves are sent out, bounce back off an object, and are detected again. The Coast Guard's radar system did not normally track ships near Bligh Reef in a reliable way.

To add to the danger, the *Exxon Valdez* was traveling outside of the **sea lanes**. A sea lane is the route that ships usually take. On the night of March 23, there had been reports of icebergs in the sea lanes. To avoid them, the ship left the lanes. Later, the crew failed to return the ship to its original route.

Icebergs can cause major damage to ships.

The ship had requested permission from the Coast Guard to switch lanes. The Coast Guard gave permission, but it soon lost radar contact with the ship. Many believe that if contact had not been lost, the Coast Guard could have warned the captain and crew that the ship was getting too close to the reef.

Timeline of the *Exxon Valdez* Oil Spill

March 23, 1989, shortly after 9:00 p.m.
The *Exxon Valdez* leaves Valdez, Alaska.

Valdez

March 24, 12:04 a.m.
The *Exxon Valdez* is grounded on Bligh Reef.

To help cut costs, the oil company hired smaller crews on their ships. Too few crew members were working on the *Exxon Valdez*. The crew worked longer hours to make up for being shorthanded. They were tired, which clouded their judgment and slowed their reactions.

May 18

Oil has spread 470 miles (750 km) from spill site.

March 30

Oil has spread 90 miles (145 km) from spill site.

March 27

A storm with powerful winds spreads the oil.

When the ship struck the reef, response from the coast was delayed. A crew member and the captain tried to move the *Exxon Valdez* from the reef. This only made the situation worse. Some argue the captain did not perform his duty properly. For one thing, moving the ship could cause more damage. A cluster of bad decisions and bad luck combined to cause the *Exxon Valdez* disaster.

Crew members had been working 12- to 14-hour shifts on the *Exxon Valdez*.

Some people blamed Captain Joseph Hazelwood for the disaster.

Causes of Major Accidents

Major disasters are caused by many factors working together. Those who study accidents, whether oil spills or plane crashes, see a pattern. Equipment failures combine with human error to make things worse. Each factor by itself may seem small. But together, they become one major issue. For the *Exxon Valdez*, better vessel-tracking radar and a well-rested crew could have lessened— or helped avoid—disaster.

Many smaller problems added up to cause major trouble in the environment surrounding the spill site.

Researchers continue to study the effects of the *Exxon Valdez* oil spill today.

CHAPTER 4

Responsibility

After the spill, many people looked for someone to blame. Courts assigned legal responsibility. Both the ship's captain and the oil company had to pay fines and spend time helping the community.

In 2010, an oil spill in the Gulf of Mexico surpassed the damage done by the *Exxon Valdez*. Researchers of both spills are still trying to understand what went wrong, and how to prevent more oil spills in the future.

Oil from the *Exxon Valdez* spill can still be found under the layers of sand of some beaches.

Existing Problems

Ten months before the spill in Prince William Sound, there was a meeting in Arizona. Oil executives were getting together to discuss business. One of the things discussed was the possibility of an oil spill. A spill in the middle of Prince William Sound, they decided, would be disastrous. Less than one year later, they were proven correct.

A researcher collects mussels from Prince William Sound in 2001. Even years later, the oil spill affects life in the surrounding area.

Unfortunately, other serious oil spills have occurred since the *Exxon Valdez*, including the 2010 BP spill in the Gulf of Mexico.

The 2010 BP oil spill in the Gulf of Mexico released almost 20 times as much oil as the *Exxon Valdez* spill.

A few smaller spills had happened in the sound before. Oil companies tried to make the problems seem less serious than they were. The companies also failed to provide equipment that could be used to clean up an oil spill. Companies sometimes promised equipment. Then they would vote in meetings not to spend money on it.

The Trans Alaska Pipeline transports oil 800 miles (1,300 kilometers) across Alaska.

The Trans Alaska Pipeline has been in use since 1977.

Broken Promises

The Chugach are a Native group living in the area around Prince William Sound. When oil was discovered in Alaska, the Trans Alaska Pipeline was built to transport it. The pipeline had to travel through Chugach land. The Chugach made a deal with oil companies that allowed the use of their land. In return, oil companies promised to use ships with the best radar available. Oil carriers would also be **escorted**, or helped, by tugboats through narrow and dangerous spots. As the *Exxon Valdez* spill shows, such promises were not really kept.

After the spill, much of the sea life that the locals depended on was killed. The populations of two fish—herring and salmon—were particularly important. These fish became difficult to find. It was even harder to sell them. People did not want to purchase fish from a polluted place. The Chugach Natives lost money. Their way of life was changed forever.

Commercial fishing is an important part of the economy in Prince William Sound.

41

The Long Term

Has Prince William Sound recovered from the spill? That's a tricky question. Natural areas are always adapting. It can be difficult to know if a specific issue relates to the spill or natural changes. Today, the ecosystem of Prince William Sound is fully functional. But it is different than it was in 1989. Scientists wonder why the herring have not returned. How will the region continue to change in the years to come? Time will tell. ★

Legally, most of the blame for the spill was placed upon Exxon Corporation.

Workers continued to find oil-covered rocks in Prince William Sound 15 years after the disaster.

Amount of oil carried by *Exxon Valdez* on March 23: 53.1 million gal. (201 million L)

Amount of oil spilled: 11 million gal. (41.6 million L)

Amount of oil recovered: Less than 10 percent

Amount of coastline covered by oil: 1,300 mi. (2,100 km)

Amount of ocean covered: 11,000 sq. mi. (28,500 sq km)

Rate at which the remaining oil is disappearing: Less than 4 percent each year

Number of seabirds that died as a direct result of the spill: 250,000

Cost of repairs to *Exxon Valdez* after the accident: $30 million

Did you find the truth?

(F) The *Exxon Valdez* never sailed again after the 1989 spill.

(T) Oil companies made a deal with the Chugach to use their land.

Resources

Books

Beech, Linda Ward. *The Exxon Valdez's Deadly Oil Spill*. New York: Bearport Publishing, 2007.

Ditchfield, Christin. *Oil*. New York: Children's Press, 2002.

Farndon, John. *Oil*. New York: DK, 2007.

Faust, Daniel R. *Sinister Sludge: Oil Spills and the Environment*. New York: PowerKids Press, 2009.

Margulies, Phillip. *The Exxon Valdez Oil Spill*. New York: Rosen Central, 2003.

Ollhoff, Jim. *Alaska*. Edina, MN: ABDO Publishing Company, 2010.

Sutherland, Jonathan, and Diane Canwell. *Container Ships and Oil Tankers*. Pleasantville, NY: Gareth Stevens Publishing, 2008.

Woods, Michael, and Mary B. Woods. *Environmental Disasters*. Minneapolis: Lerner Publications Company, 2008.

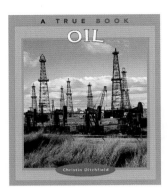

Organizations and Web Sites

EPA: No Water off a Duck's Back
www.epa.gov/owow/NPS/kids/ducksbackoil.html
Learn how oil harms waterbirds.

National Geographic: Exxon Valdez Spill
http://channel.nationalgeographic.com/series/final-report/3416/Overview
Watch a short clip and see photos of the oil spill.

National Wildlife Federation: Voices from the Exxon Valdez Oil Spill: "The Day the Water Died"
www.nwf.org/Oil-Spill/Effects-on-Wildlife/Compare-Exxon-Valdez-and-BP-Oil-Spills/Day-the-Water-Died-Report.aspx
Learn more about the oil spill's impact on wildlife and people.

Places to Visit

Prince William Sound Science Center
300 Breakwater Avenue
Cordova, AK 99574
(907) 424-5800
www.pwssc.org
Learn more about Prince William Sound through educational programs offered by this science center.

Valdez Museum & Historical Archive: The Exxon Valdez Oil Spill
217 Egan Drive
Valdez, AK 99686
(907) 835-2764
www.valdezmuseum.org
Explore this exhibit, and learn more about the oil spill and cleanup efforts.

Important Words

barge (BARJ) — a long boat with a flat bottom

booms (BOOMZ) — floating barriers used to keep oil from spreading

commercial (kuh-MUR-shuhl) — having to do with business or making money

escorted (ESS-kor-tid) — led, or helped along

grounded (GROUND-id) — became stranded by striking the shore, a reef, or the bottom of shallow water

kelp (KELP) — large, brown seaweed

radar (RAY-dar) — the use of radio waves to track objects

sea lanes (SEE-laynz) — the routes ships are expected to take

sound (SOUND) — body of water between two larger bodies of water or between an island and the mainland

spring tides (SPRING TYDEZ) — unusually high tides that occur during full or new moons

Index

Page numbers in **bold** indicate illustrations

Alyeska Pipeline Service Company, 13
animals, 20, **22–23**, **24**, **35**, **38**

bacteria, **21**
birds, **22**, **23**, 24, 35
Bligh Reef, 7, 8, 9, 15, 30, **32**, 34
booms, **19**
BP oil spill, **39**

causes, 29, 30–34, 35, 37
chemicals, **18**
Chignik, Alaska, 10
Chugach people, 40, 41
cleanup, **11**, **12**, **16**, 17, **18**, **19**, **20**, **22**, **23**, 24, **28**, 39
Coast Guard, 30, 32
coastline, **10**, **11**, **12**, **13**, **20**, **25**, **28**
commercial fishing, 25, **41**
controlled burning, 18
crew members, 29, 31, 33, 34, 35

damage, 7, 8, **9**, 15, 20–21, **22**, 24, 25, **27**, **31**, 34, **35**, **36**, **38**, **42**

economy, 25, **41**
Exxon Corporation, 17, 27, 33, 42

fines, 37
fish, 19, 24, 25, **41**, 42
fungi, 21

grounding, **6**, 7–8, 9, 11, **14**, **15**, **32**, **33**

Hazelwood, Joseph, 9, **34**, 37
herring, 41, 42

icebergs, **31**

map, **8**

oil, **6**, 7, **8**, **9**, **10**, **11**, **12**, **13**, **15**, **16**, 17, **18**, **19**, **20**, 21, **22**, 23, **24**, 25, 27, **28**, **33**, **35**, 37, 38, **39**, **40**, **42**
oil companies, 13, 17, 27, 33, 37, 38–39, 40, 42

pipelines, 13, **40**
plants, 19, 20, 22
pressure washing, **16**, **20**–21, 22
Prince William Sound, 8, **10**, **11**, **25**, 26, 30, **38**–39, 40, **41**, **42**

radar, **30**, 32, 35, 40
reef. See Bligh Reef.
repairs, **26–27**
rescue, 13–**14**
researchers, 35, **36**, 37, **38**
response barge, 13

salmon, 24, **41**
sea lanes, 31–32
seals, **24**
sea otters, 24
SeaRiver Maritime company, 27
shoreline. See coastline.
skimmers, 19
spring tides, 11, 12
storms, 10, **11**, 18, 33

timeline, **32–33**
tourism, **25**
Trans Alaska Pipeline, **40**
tugboats, 15, 17, 40

Valdez, Alaska, 7, 32

waves, 11, 12, 18
winds, 10, 33
workers, **11**, **12**, **13**, **16**, **19**, **20**, 21, **22**, **23**, **28**, **33**, **42**

About the Author

Peter Benoit is educated as a mathematician but has many other interests. He has taught and tutored high school and college students for many years, mostly in math and science. He also runs summer workshops for writers and students of literature. Mr. Benoit has also written more than 2,000 poems. His life has been one committed to learning. He lives in Greenwich, New York.